The Cure for Sorrow

ALSO BY JAN RICHARDSON

Circle of Grace
Through the Advent Door
In the Sanctuary of Women
In Wisdom's Path
Night Visions
Sacred Journeys

THE
CURE
for
SORROW

A Book *of* Blessings
for Times *of* Grief

JAN RICHARDSON

Wanton Gospeller Press
ORLANDO, FLORIDA

janrichardson.com   wantongospeller.com

FOR OUR FAMILY

————————

When the shattering world.
Then your sheltering heart.

When the sorrowing way.
Then your encircling grace.

When the unbearable dark.
Then your comfort, your light.

When the empty, the ache.
Then your welcoming door.

When you.
Then this blessing,
this grateful,
this thanks.

Contents

THE SWEETNESS THAT REMAINS
Solace Blessings

WHAT FIRE COMES TO SING IN YOU
Blessings of Hope

Acknowledgments

It is telling that a book that arises from such deep grief should be infused with so many exquisite graces. I am grateful to all who have been bearers of these graces and who have made a difference to the book and to me. Among them are Peg Carlson-Hoffman and Chuck Hoffman, Jim Knipper, Brenda Lewis, Karen Weatherford, Maru Ladròn de Guevara, the Richardson and Doles families, and everyone at Infusion Tea in College Park.

I wrote many of these blessings during a sojourn in Ireland, a place that has held much solace for me. In particular, the hospitality and good cheer I found among the kind folks in the town of Kenmare came as a wondrous gift as I worked on this book.

My extraordinary editor and friend Christianne Squires has blessed me in both these roles with her wisdom and heart.

I am forever grateful for my husband, Garrison Doles, who was grace embodied. His life continues to be a blessing, and his spirit sings through every page.

And to you, deep gratitude and every grace.

Introduction

It did not go as we anticipated.

At 4 a.m., the neurosurgeon entered the waiting room where our family had been keeping vigil for my husband. Gary had gone into surgery that afternoon to repair a brain aneurysm discovered several months earlier. He had experienced no symptoms of the aneurysm; it was spotted in the process of checking out something else that proved not to be a problem. *How fortunate*, we had thought. *How providential.* The aneurysm had been found; the treatment options were clear and low-risk; life could return to normal, all the more graced for our knowing what a potential disaster we had escaped.

The surgeon should have emerged many hours earlier to tell us everything had gone well. Instead, he sat down across from me and said, *It did not go as we anticipated.* There was a clot; there was a massive stroke. Though the surgeon spoke words of hope, hope began to run out in the days that followed. Complications accumulated, then cascaded. Gary never regained consciousness. Nearly three weeks after his initial surgery, just as the season of Advent was beginning, Gary died.

We had been married not four years.

Believing What a Blessing Can Do

At the time of Gary's death, I had been composing blessings for years. I have a persistent fascination with this ancient literary form that holds some of the most beautiful writings of the Jewish and Christian traditions. Whether offered in the formality of liturgy or woven through the rhythms of daily life, blessings invoke God's care for all manner of people, activities, and objects, illuminating the presence of the sacred that inhabits and intertwines with the ordinary.

In the rending that came with Gary's death, I continued to write blessings. As everything about my life changed, I wrote blessings still. Looking back, I sense I was searching for confirmation of what I had long believed about blessings. At the core of that belief lived the conviction that a blessing conveys God's desire for our wholeness and that it holds the ability to open us to the presence of God in any circumstance.

In the wake of Gary's death, I needed, more than ever, to believe in what a blessing can do.

Although we often equate blessings with God's benevolence, thinking that they constitute a sign of God's favor in the form of prosperity and abundance, they often work in ways quite contrary to such a notion. I have come to see with greater and greater clarity that a blessing is at its most potent in times of disaster, devastation, and loss. When God's providence seems most difficult to find, a blessing helps us perceive the grace that threads through our lives.

A blessing does not explain away our loss or justify devastation. It does not make light of grief or provide a simple fix for the rending. It does not compel us to "move on." Instead, a blessing meets us in the place of our deepest loss. In that place, it offers us a glimpse of wholeness and claims that wholeness here and now. A blessing helps us to keep breathing—to abide this moment, and the next moment, and the one after that.

A good blessing possesses something of what Celtic folk have long called a *thin place*, a space where the veil between worlds becomes permeable, and heaven and earth meet. In a thin place, God is not somehow more present, more *there* than in other places. Instead, a thin place enables us to open our eyes and hearts to the presence of God that goes with us always. A blessing invites us to this same opening, that we might recognize and receive the help of the One who created us in love and encompasses us when we are at our most broken.

Like a thin place, a blessing can help us perceive how heaven infuses earth, inextricable from daily life, even when that life is marked by pain. In the midst of grief, when our loss can make the boundary between worlds feel horribly solid, insurmountable, and permanent, this comes as a particular grace.

In the Rending, in Solace, in Hope

The Cure for Sorrow holds layers of blessings. The book includes blessings I wrote before Gary died—blessings he saw and talked about with me, as he always did, before I released them into the world. I wrote most of those blessings for my blog *The Painted Prayerbook*, where I have offered reflections in response to the

Scripture readings from week to week. I have been struck by how these blessings I wrote before Gary's death have so often held solace for me on this side of his dying. I take this as a testament to the ability of a blessing to work beyond the boundaries of time.

Some of these blessings I wrote in the days and weeks after Gary died, including one for his memorial service—the most wrenching blessing I have ever composed. Many of these blessings are recent, written as I have begun to trace the outlines of a different life, nearly three years now since Gary's death.

The layers of blessings are a testimony to how Gary's life, and our life together, has so deeply formed me. In a mystery that comes as grace in the still-intense grief, the life we have shared continues to be a place of blessing that influences what—and how—I create. This is reflected in the blessings that inhabit these pages.

The blessings are gathered into three sections:

Getting the News: Blessings in the Rending. These blessings speak to the immediacy of grief and the intensity of the fracturing that attends loss in whatever form it visits us, including losses other than the physical death of someone we love. This section also acknowledges the presence of complicated emotions that can weave through our mourning, such as anger and fear.

The Sweetness That Remains: Solace Blessings. The blessings in this section invite us to open ourselves to the grace that lives in times of devastation. In our deepest grief, we can find it difficult to allow ourselves to receive this grace and the comfort it offers us. These blessings ask us to accept this solace and to enter into the rhythms that will bring our deepest healing, even as we continue to live with the pain of loss.

What Fire Comes to Sing in You: Blessings of Hope. These blessings testify to the tenacity of hope—how it persists in finding us and working its way into our lives even when we feel hopeless. These blessings ask us to see our brokenness in light of the brokenness of the world—to let our shared brokenness become a bridge of engagement and response that leads us to new connections, unexpected paths, and doorways we could hardly have imagined.

Although the blessings are divided into these sections, it is crucial, of course, to remember that grieving is not an orderly process. Grief is the least linear thing I know. Hardly a tidy progression of stages, grief tends to be unruly. It works with the most raw and elemental forces in us, which makes it unpredictable and wild. Grief resists our attempts to force it along a prescribed path. It propels us in directions we had not planned to go. It causes what we treated as solid to give way. It opens new seams of mourning in places we thought settled. It spirals us back through layers of sorrow we thought we had dealt with.

Because of the spiral quality of grief, there is considerable overlap between the sections of this book. This is a reflection and honoring of how grief moves in anything but a straight line. Solace reaches out to us even as loss rends us. Deeper rending can happen even as solace begins to heal us. Hope visits us in the most hidden layers of our sorrow. Though grief's unpredictability can sometimes daunt us, this intertwining of rending, solace, and hope is one of its greatest gifts.

GRIEF, PARTICULARLY

Grief is piercingly particular. There is hardly any limit to the ways loss will find us, entering into our lives not only through the death of someone we love but also through the myriad other ways life can wrest from us what we have held dear. When grief does find us—however it finds us—it shapes itself precisely to the details of our lives. It fits itself to our habits and routines, our relationships, our priorities, what we have organized our lives around—all that makes us who we are in this world. Because of this, no one will know our grief as we do. No one will inhabit it in the same way we do. No one will entirely understand what it is like to live with our specific shattering.

There is something beautiful about this. Our particular grief reflects the particular wonder of what we had—a grace that visited our life in a way designed especially for us. Yet this very quality can compound our grief because it leaves us feeling so alone. One of grief's most insidious aspects lies in how isolating it can become. This aspect of grief calls for intentionality from us: that we resist grief's capacity to cut us off from those around us at the time we need them most.

For all its particularity, the heartrending and hopeful reality of grief is that it is universal. It hardly needs saying that in our living, each of us will know loss. Though we will never know how it feels to live in someone else's loss, grief has the capacity to connect us even across deep divides. Fierce loss can forge fierce connections. Grief holds the power to help us recognize our shared fragility and also to call forth our mutual resilience as we meet one another in sometimes unspeakable pain.

In *The Cure for Sorrow*—the second in a series of books of blessings that began with *Circle of Grace*—I offer blessings from my path of piercing grief. This book is not a systematic compendium that addresses every kind of grief. It is, instead, more like a constellation. From the deep shadows of my own sorrow, I offer blessings like votive flames, praying they will lend some light to your own path. I offer these lights not to show you the way—you will find the way for yourself—but in the hope that the light will help you perceive the grace that already travels with you.

Whatever the cause of your grief, may these lights help you know you do not go alone.

GETTING THE NEWS

—————

Blessings in the Rending

BLESSING FOR GETTING THE NEWS

I don't know
how it will be
for you.

For me,
when the news came—
when it sat down
across from me in the
waiting room
at 4 a.m.,
wearing scrubs and
speaking words awful
and full of
strangeness—
it came with
a humming in
my head,
an endless, echoing buzzing
that would never
entirely leave.

I can hardly tell you
the words the news used—
others would piece that
together for me,
later—
but I can tell you that
in the humming,
a whole other conversation
was happening.

In that conversation,
I remember wanting
to appear calm
while the world
was beginning the rending
from which it
never would return.

In that conversation,
I remember wanting
to be the wife
who could withstand
what the news
was saying to me,
even as I could
hardly hear it.

In that conversation,
I remember wanting
to ask if someone could please
get me a blanket already
because I was shaking
so hard I thought
I would shatter.

I do not know
how it will be
for you.
But when
the news comes,
may it be attended
by every grace,

including the ones
you will not be able
to see now.

When the news comes,
may there be hands
to enfold and bless,
even when
you cannot receive
their blessing now.

When the news comes,
may the humming
in your head
give way to song,
even if it will be
long and long
before you can
hear it,

before you can
comprehend the love
that latched onto you
in the rending—
the love that bound itself to you
even as it began its leaving
and has never
let you go.

Blessing for My First Day as a Widow

Because I need
to go back
and tell her
what she could not have
heard anyone else say.

Weep.
Scream.
Wail if you want.

There was a reason
the ancients told us
to rend our clothes
after a death,
to cover our heads
with ashes.

They knew that
keeping it together
is overrated.

Do not pass by
the opportunity
to lament
what is forever gone
from here.
It is an honoring
of what has been.
It makes room
for what

may be—
the life you cannot imagine
from here, in this place
where you can barely
plan two minutes
at a time.

The weeping will
clear your vision.

People will want to help
when you cannot know
what could help,
what could ever make
the world stop falling away
from beneath your feet,
from your heart that
will never be here,
will never beat here,
in the same way.

Let them help.

There will be days
the tears will begin
as soon as your feet
hit the floor.

There will be days
the tears will not wait
as long as that.

Let the tears come,
every time.

Then make breakfast.

Let yourself lean into
the circle of your closest ones,
your dearest ones,
and do not fret
for the friends you have
no energy for.
The kind ones
will keep,
will wait
while you learn
how to live
all over again.

I should tell you
this is all provisional,
because the point is that
from here you will
have to wake up
every day
and ask yourself
what you need.

It will change.

It will change again.

It will keep changing,
and so you will have

to keep asking
the question.
You will not always
know the answer.
You will not always
even want to ask.

Ask.

I should also tell you
this blessing is incomplete
because, finally, you will
have to find it yourself,
will have to create it
in the way that only
you can figure out
as you stumble along—
I won't say *forward*,
because your path
will not go
in a straight line.

But it's true,
you know.
You will move along
in ways you cannot see
from here,
cannot envision
even in the dreams
that make their way to you
through your most painful
nights.

I don't know how
to end this blessing.
I am still finding it
myself.
But I am here to tell you
there is grace—

my heart,
is there ever grace.

So keep your eyes open,
is all I'm saying.
Try not to miss it.

WHERE YOUR SONG BEGINS AGAIN

Beloved,
I could not bear it
if this blessing ended
with the final beat
of your heart,

if it left
with the last breath
that bore you away
from here.

I could not stand
the silence,
the stillness
where all
had once been song,
had been story,
had been the cadenced liturgy
of your life.

So let it be
that this blessing
will abide
in the pulse
that moves us
from this moment
to the next.

Let it be
that you will breathe

in us here bereft
but beloved still.

Let it be
that you will make your home
in the chamber
of our heart

where your story
does not cease,
where your words
take flesh anew,
where your song
begins again.

Written for Gary's memorial service.

BLESSING FOR THE BROKENHEARTED

There is no remedy for love but to love more.
        —Henry David Thoreau

Let us agree
for now
that we will not say
the breaking
makes us stronger
or that it is better
to have this pain
than to have done
without this love.

Let us promise
we will not
tell ourselves
time will heal
the wound,
when every day
our waking
opens it anew.

Perhaps for now
it can be enough
to simply marvel
at the mystery
of how a heart
so broken
can go on beating,

as if it were made
for precisely this—

as if it knows
the only cure for love
is more of it,

as if it sees
the heart's sole remedy
for breaking
is to love still,

as if it trusts
that its own
persistent pulse
is the rhythm
of a blessing
we cannot
begin to fathom
but will save us
nonetheless.

GOD OF THE LIVING

*"Now he is God not of the dead, but of the living;
for to him all of them are alive."*
—Luke 20:38

When the wall
between the worlds
is too firm,
too close.

When it seems
all solidity
and sharp edges.

When every morning
you wake as if
flattened against it,
its forbidding presence
fairly pressing the breath
from you
all over again.

Then may you be given
a glimpse
of how weak the wall

and how strong what stirs
on the other side,

breathing with you
and blessing you
still,

forever bound to you
but freeing you
into this living,
into this world
so much wider
than you ever knew.

It Is Hard Being Wedded to the Dead

It is hard
being wedded
to the dead;
they make different claims,
offer comforts
that do not feel comfortable
at the first.

They do not let you
remain numb.
Neither do they allow you
to languish forever
in your grief.

They will safeguard
your sorrow
but will not permit
that it should become
your new country,
your home.

They knew you first
in joy,
in delight,
and though they will be patient
when you travel
by other roads,
it is here
that they will wait
for you,

here they can best
be found,

where the river runs deep
with gladness,
the water over each stone
singing your
unforgotten name.

In the Cleaving

"I will put you in a cleft of the rock, and I will
cover you with my hand until I have passed by."
    —Exodus 33:22

Believe me,
I know how
this blessing looks:
like it is
leaving you,
like it is
walking away
while you stand there,
feeling the press
of every sharp edge,
every jagged corner
in this fearsome hollow
that holds you.

I know how hard it is
to abide this blessing
when some part of it
remains always hidden
from view
even as it sees you
from every angle,
inhabits your
entire being,
calls you
by your name.

I know the anguish
of vision that comes
in such fragments,
the terrible wonder
of glory that arrives
only in glimpses.

So I am not here
to make excuses
for this blessing,
for how it turns
its face from us
when we need
to see it most.

But I want to believe
it will always
find its way to us
when we are in the place
made by cleaving—
the space left
by what is torn apart
even as it is joined
in the fierce union
that comes only
in the fissure.

I want to be unafraid
to turn toward
this blessing
that binds itself to us
even in the rending,

this blessing
that unhinges us
even as it
makes us whole.

Blessing for the Dailiness of Grief

Sorry I am
to say it,
but it is here,
most likely,
you will know the rending
most deeply.

It will take your breath away,
how the grieving waits for you
in the most ordinary moments.

It will wake
with your waking.

It will
sit itself down
with you at the table,
inhabiting the precise shape
of the emptiness
across from you.

It will walk down the street
with you
in the form of
no hand reaching out
to take yours.

It will stand alongside you
in every conversation,
nearly unbearable

in its silence
that fairly screams.

It will
brush its teeth
with you at night
and climb into bed
with you
when finally
you let go
of this day.

Even as it goes
always with you,
it will still manage
to startle you with
its presence,
causing you to weep
when you enter
the empty kitchen
in the morning,
when you spread fresh sheets
on the bed you shared,
when you walk out
through the door
alone
and pass back through it
likewise.

It is here
you will know it best—
in the moments

that made up the rhythm
of your days,
that fashioned the litany
of your life,
the togethering
you will never know
in the same way again.

But I will tell you
it is here, too,
that your solace lies.
It will wait for you
in those same moments
that stun you
with their sorrow.

I cannot tell you how,
but it will not cease
to carry you
in the cadence that has
forever altered
but whose echo will persist
with a stubbornness
that will surprise you,
bearing you along,
breathing with you still
through the terrible
and exquisite
ordinary days.

Blessing for Coming Home to an Empty House

I know
how every time you return,
you call out
in greeting
to the one
who is not there,
how you lift your voice
not in habit
but in honor
of the absence
so fierce
it has become
its own force.

I know
how the hollow
of the house
echoes in your chest,
how the emptiness
you enter
matches the ache
you carry with you
always.

I know
there are days
when the only thing
more brave than leaving
this house
is coming back to it.

So on those days,
may there be a door
in the emptiness
through which a welcome
waits for you.

On those days,
may you be surprised
by the grace
that gathers itself
within this space.

On those days,
may the delight
that made a home here
find its way to you again,
not merely in memory
but in hope,

so that every word
ever spoken in kindness
circles back to meet you,

so that you may hear
what still sings to you
within these walls,

so that you may know
the love
that dreams with you here
when finally
you give yourself
to rest—

the love
that rises with you,
faithful like the dawn
that never fails
to come.

BLESSING IN THE ANGER

You might think
it would come
with a clamoring,
a clashing,
clanging around
in heavy boots,
hollering and
hot in its rage.

What it does not
tell you
is how quietly
it loves to bear itself
toward us,
hardly uttering a word
until it shows up
with such suddenness—
splintering into
the broken pieces
on the floor,
the dent
in the wall,
the hole torn
in what had once
been whole—

and no one there
to witness
the damage,
no one

to sweep away
the shards

(which is why
the anger comes
at all).

Let it be
no stranger.

Let it be
visitor,
teacher,
guide.

Let it be
messenger,
come to tell us
what we most
need to know,
hard though its words
may be to hear.

Trust,
even when you
cannot believe it,
that it will carry
its own consolations,
that it knows
what to do
with what
has shattered.

Trust
that the other face
of anger
is courage,
that it holds the key
to your secret strength,
that the fire it offers
will light your way.

BLESSING THE QUESTIONS

Let them come:
the questions
that storm through
the crack in the world.

Let them come:
the questions
that crawl through
the hole in your heart.

Let them come:
the questions
in anguish,
the questions
in tears.

Let them come:
the questions
in rage,
the questions
in fear.

Let them come:
the questions
that whisper themselves
so slow,

the questions
that arrive with
breathtaking speed,

the questions
that never entirely leave,
the questions
that bring
more questions still.

Let them come:
the questions
that haunt you
in shadowy hours,

the questions
that visit
in deepest night,

the questions
that draw you
into rest,
into dream,

the questions
that stir
the wakening
world.

The Blessing You Should Not Tell Me

Do not tell me
there will be a blessing
in the breaking,
that it will ever
be a grace
to wake into this life
so altered,
this world
so without.

Do not tell me
of the blessing
that will come
in the absence.

Do not tell me
that what does not
kill me
will make me strong
or that God will not
send me more than I
can bear.

Do not tell me
this will make me
more compassionate,
more loving,
more holy.

Do not tell me
this will make me
more grateful for what
I had.

Do not tell me
I was lucky.

Do not even tell me
there will be a blessing.

Give me instead
the blessing
of breathing with me.

Give me instead
the blessing
of sitting with me
when you cannot think
of what to say.

Give me instead
the blessing
of asking about him—
how we met
or what I loved most
about the life
we have shared;
ask for a story
or tell me one
because a story is, finally,
the only place on earth
he lives now.

If you could know
what grace lives
in such a blessing,
you would never cease
to offer it.

If you could glimpse
the solace and sweetness
that abide there,
you would never wonder
if there was a blessing
you could give
that would be better
than this—
the blessing of
your own heart
opened
and beating
with mine.

BLESSING THAT COMES TO YOU IN PIECES

In the desolate
      when
(at night, say)

at its most
(brilliant?)
(brittle?)

      never and
ever you will again

      anywhere but here.

Tell me again
            that time you

in the last song
you

or how you
                  tenderness
would always

Promise
(seriously)
(truly)

and you still

It wouldn't have made
any
so let it
let it

O my
(love?)
(life?)

and the
dreams that
between us now.

I Am Writing This Blessing

Instead of lying
in bed with him
on this summer afternoon,
I am writing
this blessing.

Instead of watching
how the light falls across us,
I am writing
this blessing.

Instead of tracing
the curve of his back,
I am writing
this blessing.

Instead of placing
my head on his chest,
I am writing
this blessing.

Instead of meeting
his mouth with my mouth,
I am writing
this blessing.

Instead of twining
my legs through his,
I am writing
this blessing.

Instead,
instead,
instead,
I am writing
this blessing still.

Blessing for Falling into a New Layer of Grief

You thought
you had hit
every layer possible,
that you had found
the far limit
of your sorrow,
your grief.

Now the world falls
from beneath your feet
all over again,
as if the wound
were opening
for the first time,
only now with
an ache you recognize
as ancient.

Here is the time
for kindness—
your own, to yourself—
as you fall
and fall,
as you land hard
in this layer
that lies deeper than
you ever imagined
you could go.

Think of it as
a secret room—
this space
that has opened
before you,
that has opened
inside you,
though it may look
sharp in every corner
and sinister
no matter where
you turn.

Think of it as
a hidden chamber
in your heart
where you can stay
as long as you need,
where you will
find provision
you never wanted
but on which
your life will now
depend.

I want to tell you
there is treasure
even here—
that the sharp lines
that so match your scars
will lead
to solace,

that this space
that feels so foreign
will become for you
a shelter.

So let yourself fall.
It will not be
the last time,
but do not let this be
cause for fear.

These are the rooms
around which your
new home will grow—
the home of your heart,
the home of your life
that welcomes you
with such completeness,
opening and
opening and
opening itself to you,
no part of you
turned away.

STUBBORN BLESSING

*A Canaanite woman . . . came out and started
shouting, "Have mercy on me, Lord, Son of David;
my daughter is tormented by a demon."*
            —Matthew 15:22

Don't tell me no.
I have seen you
feed the thousands,
seen miracles spill
from your hands
like water, like wine,
seen you with circles
and circles of crowds
pressed around you
and not one soul
turned away.

Don't start with me.

I am saying
you can close the door,
but I will keep knocking.
You can go silent,
but I will keep shouting.
You can tighten the circle,
but I will trace a bigger one
around you,
around the life of my child,
who will tell you
no one surpasses a mother
for stubbornness.

I am saying
I know what you
can do with crumbs
and I am claiming mine,
every morsel and scrap
you have up your sleeve.

Unclench your hand,
your heart.
Let the scraps fall
like manna,
like mercy
for the life
of my child,
the life of
the world.

Don't you tell me no.

Blessing in a Time of Violence

Which is to say
this blessing
is always.

Which is to say
there is no place
this blessing
does not long
to cry out
in lament,
to weep its words
in sorrow,
to scream its lines
in sacred rage.

Which is to say
there is no day
this blessing ceases
to whisper
into the ear
of the dying,
the despairing,
the terrified.

Which is to say
there is no moment
this blessing refuses
to sing itself
into the heart
of the hated
and the hateful,

the victim
and the victimizer,
with every last
ounce of hope
it has.

Which is to say
there is none
that can stop it,
none that can
halt its course,
none that will
still its cadence,
none that will
delay its rising,
none that can keep it
from springing forth
from the mouths of us
who hope,
from the hands of us
who act,
from the hearts of us
who love,
from the feet of us
who will not cease
our stubborn, aching
marching, marching

until this blessing
has spoken
its final word,

until this blessing
has breathed
its benediction
in every place,
in every tongue:

Peace.
Peace.
Peace.

Jacob's Blessing

*Jacob was left alone; and a man wrestled with him
until daybreak.*
        —Genesis 32:24

If this blessing were easy,
anyone could claim it.
As it is,
I am here to tell you
that it will take some work.

This is the blessing
that visits you
in the struggling,
in the wrestling,
in the striving.

This is the blessing
that comes
after you have left
everything behind,
after you have stepped out,
after you have crossed
into that realm
beyond every landmark
you have known.

This is the blessing
that takes all night
to find.

It's not that this blessing
is so difficult,
as if it were not filled
with grace
or with the love
that lives
in every line.

It's simply that
it requires you
to want it,
to ask for it,
to place yourself
in its path.
It demands that you
stand to meet it
when it arrives,
that you stretch yourself
in ways you didn't know
you could move,
that you agree
to not give up.

So when this blessing comes,
borne in the hands
of the difficult angel
who has chosen you,
do not let go.
Give yourself
into its grip.

It will wound you,
but I tell you
there will come a day
when what felt to you
like limping

was something more
like dancing
as you moved into
the cadence
of your new
and blessed name.

Blessing the Desert

Ask me what
this blessing sounds like
and I will tell you
about the wind
that hollows everything
it finds.

I will tell you
about locusts
who chose this night
to offer their awful,
rasping song.

I will tell you
about rock faces
and how it sounds
when what was sturdy
and solid
suddenly shears away.

But give me long enough,
and I will tell you also
how beneath the wind,
a silence,

not of absence
or of agony
that leaves all speechless
and stricken
when it comes,

but of rest,
of dreaming,

of the seed
that knows its season

and the wordless
canticle of stars
that will not cease
their singing
even when we cannot bear
to hear.

THE SWEETNESS
THAT REMAINS

Solace Blessings

Blessing the House of the Heart

If you could see
how this blessing
shimmers inside you,
you would never wonder
whether there will be
light enough,
time enough,
room enough for you.

If you could see
the way this blessing
has inscribed itself
on every wall
of your heart,
writing its shining line
across every doorway,
tracing the edge
of every window
and table
and hall—

if you could see this,
you would never question
where home is
or whether it has
a welcome for you.

This blessing wishes
to give you
a glimpse.

It will not tell you
it has been waiting.
It will not tell you
it has been keeping watch.
It would not
want you to know
just how long
it has been holding
this quiet vigil
for you.

It simply wants you
to see what it sees,
wants you to know
what it knows—
how this blessing
already blazes in you,
illuminating every corner
of your broken
and beautiful heart.

SOLACE BLESSING

That's it.
That's all this blessing
knows how to do:

Shine your shoes.
Fill your refrigerator.
Water your plants.
Make some soup.

All the things
you cannot think
to do yourself
when the world
has come apart,
when nothing
will be normal
again.

Somehow
this blessing knows
precisely what you need,
even before
you know.

It sees what will bring
the deepest solace
for you.
It senses what will offer
the kindest grace.

And so it will step
with such quietness
into the ordinary moments
where the absence
is the deepest.

It will enter
with such tenderness
into the hours
where the sorrow
is most keen.

You do not even
have to ask.

Just leave it open—
your door,
your heart,
your day
in every aching moment
it holds.

See what solace
spills through the gaps
your sorrow has torn.

See what comfort
comes to visit,
holding out its gifts
in each compassionate hand.

Blessing in the Chaos

To all that is chaotic
in you,
let there come silence.

Let there be
a calming
of the clamoring,
a stilling
of the voices that
have laid their claim
on you,
that have made their
home in you,

that go with you
even to the
holy places
but will not
let you rest,
will not let you
hear your life
with wholeness
or feel the grace
that fashioned you.

Let what distracts you
cease.
Let what divides you
cease.
Let there come an end

to what diminishes
and demeans,
and let depart
all that keeps you
in its cage.

Let there be
an opening
into the quiet
that lies beneath
the chaos,
where you find
the peace
you did not think
possible
and see what shimmers
within the storm.

Blessing Where a Life Was Made

Bless this place
where a life
has been.

Bless this place
where a life
was made—

where two
entered the day
in the curve
of the arm,

moved through the day
in the curve of
the hours,

laid themselves down
at the end of the day
in the curve of
the body,
the belly,
the heart.

Bless this place
where two
ate together,
talked together,
danced;

where two
did the dishes,
the laundry,
the lists;

where two
worked
and dreamed
and loved.

Bless this place
and the life
left behind—
this emptiness
that is not empty,
this absence
that is not void.

Bless this place
that knows full well
what was made here,
that wears
the mark of it
always,
imprinted forever
by what passed by
in its intricate,
astonishing grace.

Blessing for Dining Alone

I know of hardly
any place
we will find ourselves
more haunted
than here.

Here
where it is hard
to say grace.

Here
where the absence
attends us with
such intimacy.

Here
where the emptiness
enters every morsel
and bitterness flavors
every bite.

Here
where we know
how aloneness
becomes its own ritual,
the unchosen practice
that alters us,
hollows us,
consumes us.

So here,
of all places,
may there be
a sweetness
that comes to you
for the savoring.

Here
may you know
yourself seen
and remembered.

Here
may you know
the table inhabited
by the persistent presence
that comes with
a stunning plenty.

Here
may you know
the blessing
that abides
in the breaking,
the Eucharist
that echoes still,
the communion
that does not end.

May it be here
at the table
that you know at last

how emptiness
becomes an altar,
how solitude
becomes a sanctuary
where we,
with deepest hunger,
say our fervent,
hopeful grace.

Blessing for Carrying Long Sorrow

When long sorrow.
When the endless
bearing of grief.
When sadness
has been waking
with you
for what seems like
forever
and going to bed with you
for what approximates
an eternity.

When your heart
has become
an ancient timepiece,
its beat measuring ages
and eons,
ticking the turning
of centuries,
and the stars
have nothing on you
for long enduring.

May there come
a moment
when time
falls away.

May there come
a space
between the beats

of your heart
when you know
your burden
carried.

May there come
a gap between
your painful breaths
when you sense
your own self
borne,
unalone in your
endless sorrowing,
no longer solitary—

as if you could
ever have been
left in your grief,
as if you could
ever have been
for one moment
abandoned to this weight,
unencompassed by the love
more ancient still
than the sorrow
you bear.

Insomnia Blessing

For you awake
in sorrow.
For you awake
in pain.
For you awake
in illness.
For you awake
in grief.

For you awake
in worry.
For you awake
in fear.
For you awake
in loneliness.
For you awake
in rage.

May peace
lay itself
beside you.
May rest
enfold you with
its grace.
May solace
breathe into
your being.
May sleep
come and call
your name.

That you will
close your eyes
in comfort.
That you will
spend this night
in peace.
That you will
give yourself
to dreaming.
That you will
waken into joy.

BLESSING OF BREATHING

That the first breath
will come without fear.

That the second breath
will come without pain.

The third breath:
that it will come without despair.

And the fourth,
without anxiety.

That the fifth breath
will come with no bitterness.

That the sixth breath
will come for joy.

Breath seven:
that it will come for love.

May the eighth breath
come for freedom.

And the ninth,
for delight.

When the tenth breath comes,
may it be for us
to breathe together,

and the next,
and the next,

until our breathing
is as one,
until our breathing
is no more.

The Sweetness That Remains
(Orange Blossom Honey Blessing)

To give you this blessing,
first I will need to tell you
about the woman who,
at the reception after
my husband's service,
handed me a jar of
orange blossom honey
on which she had written
the words,
The sweetness remains.

Then I will need to tell you how,
for nearly every morning of my life,
I have had orange blossom honey
with my breakfast.

I will need to tell you how
I grew up among orange trees,
how the scent of their blossoms
is emblazoned in my memory,
how their honey is my favorite.

My friend could not have known this
when she brought orange blossom honey
to my husband's funeral.
Nor could she have known that,
nine months later, I would find
a secret scrap on which
he had begun a song for me.

Orange blossom honey
Sweetest honey in the world
Oh my orange blossom honey
Orange blossom honey girl

Having told you these things,
I can tell you now about the blessing of
the sweetness that remains.

I can tell you
the sweetness that remains
is not a saccharine sweetness.
It is not refined.
It is not sugary or cloying.
It is not without substance.

The sweetness that remains
is terrible and wild.

The sweetness that remains
is the honey Jacob ate
from the crags of desert stones.

The sweetness that remains
is the honey Samson took
from the carcass of the lion
he had torn apart with his own hands.

The sweetness that remains
is the honey God longed to bring
out of the rocks for the wandering
children of Israel.

The sweetness that remains
is the honey John the Baptist
devoured with his locusts
in the wilderness.

Difficult sweet.
Painful sweet.
Hard-won sweet.
Desolate sweet.

Sweet that comes
to you in the desert.
Sweet that comes
to you from stones.
Sweet that lives
in the places of death.
Sweet that makes a home
in the wreck of your heart.

Did I say I would give you this blessing?

What I meant is that
you will need to tear this blessing apart
to get to the sweet.

You will need to break it open
to get to the sweet.

To get to the sweet,
you will need to turn toward
the death that stalks you.

To get to the sweet,
you will need to enter
the wilderness that calls you.

Here, look:
in the crag of the stone,
in the bones of the lion,
in the deep of the rock,
in the heart of the wilderness—

honey flowing through.

Take this blessing.
The sweetness remains.

BLESSING OF WINGS

I want to tell you
the first thing I saw here
was wings.

Not like the ones
you see in the paintings,
dazzling and ethereal—

the wings here
shine, yes,
but think of
the osprey we watched
that day,
how it flashed
in the sunlight
as it loosed itself
from the sky,

plummeting between
the two worlds
like a taloned angel,
not so much fallen
as flung,

all heart
and sinew
and nerve
as it went for
the catch it had found—
impossibly, it would seem—
from that far distance.

The wings here,
they belong
to something like that—
something that knows
how to go for the throat,

something with
piercing sight
that can find you from
that other realm,

except that here
we are so willingly caught,
carried into something
I can hardly say.

What else?

This light that
never leaves,
even when night comes—
and night does come, here—
but then the light
is more felt
than seen,
or—and I know this
is hard to fathom,
but trust me—
more heard,
like a singing brilliance
that goes straight
to your bones.

And time—
I will save that
as a surprise, but
I will say for now
you will find it both
more familiar
and more strange
than you imagined.

Keep listening
to your heartbeat,
and that will tell you
something.

I want to say
you should be at peace
about it all,
but it is hard
to find the words
for what I mean

when mostly
I want you
to know that,
of any blessing
I could give you
right now,
it would be
those wings.

Beginning with Beloved

And a voice came from heaven, "You are my Son, the Beloved."
        —Mark 1:11

Begin here:

Beloved.

Is there any other word
needs saying,
any other blessing
could compare
with this name,
this knowing?

Beloved.

Comes like a mercy
to the ear that has never
heard it.
Comes like a river
to the body that has never
seen such grace.

Beloved.

Comes holy
to the heart
aching to be new.
Comes healing

to the soul
wanting to begin
again.

Beloved.

Keep saying it,
and though it may
sound strange at first,
watch how it becomes
part of you,
how it becomes you,
as if you never
could have known yourself
anything else,
as if you could ever
have been other
than this:

Beloved.

JONAH'S BLESSING

But Jonah set out to flee . . . from the presence of the LORD.
> —Jonah 1:3

It comes as small surprise
that you would turn your back
on this blessing,
that you would run
far from the direction
in which it calls,
that you would try
to put an ocean
between yourself
and what it asks.

Something in you knows
this blessing could
swallow you whole,
no matter which way
you turn.

Hard to believe, then,
that every line of this blessing
swims in grace—
grace that, in the end,
even you
will find hard to fathom,
so swiftly does it come
and with such completeness,
encompassing all
it meets.

What to do, then,
with such a blessing
that depends so little
on us
and yet asks of us
everything?

What to do
with a blessing
that comes with
such strange provision,
every inch of it
looking like something
that will draw us
into our dying?

Trust me when I say
all it wants
is for you
to fall in,
to let yourself
find yourself
engulfed within
the curious refuge
that it holds,

and then to go
in the direction
it propels you,
following its flow
that will bear you
where you desired not,

where you dreamed not,
yet none but you
could land.

Fierce Blessing

Believe me when I say
there is nothing
this blessing would not do
to protect you,
to save you,
to encompass you.

This blessing
would stand between you
and every danger,
every evil,
every harm
and hurt.

This blessing
would dare
to wade with you
into the waters that come
offering life.

It would make
a way for you
through the waters that come
threatening death.

I cannot explain
how fierce
this blessing feels
about you,
but I can tell you

it has more than pledged
itself to you;
it would lay down
its life for you
and not once
look back in regret
nor go in sorrow
for what it has chosen
to give.

And you—
so deeply blessed,
so utterly encompassed—
what will you save
in turn?

Not because
it is owed,
but because
you cannot imagine
failing to pass along
this grace
that casts its circle
so wide,
this love
that flows
so deep
through this perilous
and precious life.

Blessing of the Wellspring

It is true
you can search
and search,
longing for
the waters you think
will slake
this parching,
will drench
the bone-dry walls
of your heart,
will wash away the dust
from which your path
through these days
is made.

A measure of quenching
may come
from your looking,
but I tell you
there is still
another wellspring
that loves this wilderness,
that has chosen it
for its home,
that has learned
how to hide itself
until the moment
of your greatest need.

It is not that it delights
in secrecy.
It is not punishing you
with patience.
It is not withholding from you
a blessing it thinks
you do not yet deserve.

It is simply
that this spring
relishes the element
of surprise,
that it loves
rising up to meet
your deeper thirst—
the one you have been
carrying all this way,
the one that
hollowed you most,
the one that,
until the waters
touched your lips,
you did not
even know
you had.

LOST BLESSING

It doesn't always
mean to go astray.
But somehow
this blessing knew
it would find you here—

here in this place
where even you
don't know where
you are.

This blessing
regrets to say
it left its compass
at home.
It is without map,
chart, GPS.
It has hardly
any sense
of direction.

This blessing
appears to be
nearly useless,
in fact.

But—
and I know
this might not be
encouraging—

it purely loves
getting lost.

This blessing
has learned to breathe
when it has left
every landmark behind,
when it has seen
its last signpost,
when dark has
begun to fall
while it is
still far from home.

This blessing
knows the prayers to say
when it has misplaced
its way,
the chants
that will help it
find the path
where it seems
no path could ever be.

This blessing
is good at finding
fellow travelers.

It loves the company
of the lost,
the wandering,
the confused,

the ones who have been
walking in circles
for days;

loves helping them
find water, shelter,
shade;

loves keeping vigil
so they can
safely rest.

The point of this blessing
is that it has
no real point.

It just wants you to know
you are not alone,
have never been,
will never be—

that it will go with you,
will wander with you
as long as you want,
as long as it takes,
gladly lost with you
until your way
appears.

Enduring Blessing

What I really want to tell you
is to just lay this blessing
on your forehead,
on your heart;
let it rest
in the palm of your hand,
because there is hardly anything
this blessing could say,
any word it could offer
to fill the hollow.

Let this blessing
work its way
into you
with its lines
that hold nearly
unspeakable lament.

Let this blessing
settle into you
with its hope
more ancient
than knowing.

Hear how this blessing
has not come alone—
how it echoes with
the voices of those
who accompany you,
who attend you in every moment,

who continually whisper
this blessing to you.

Hear how they
do not cease
to walk with you,
even when the dark
is deepest.

Hear how they
encompass you always—
breathing this blessing to you,
bearing this blessing to you
still.

THE HEALING THAT COMES

I know how long
you have been waiting
for your story to take
a different turn,
how far
you have gone in search
of what will mend you
and make you whole.

I bear no remedy,
no cure,
no miracle
for the easing
of your pain.

But I know
the medicine
that lives in a story
that has been
broken open.

I know
the healing that comes
in ceasing
to hide ourselves away
with fingers clutched
around the fragments
we think are
none but ours.

See how they fit together,
these shards
we have been carrying—
how in their meeting
they make a way
we could not
find alone.

This Brightness That You Bear

This blessing
hardly knows what to say,
speechless as it is
not simply
from grief
but from the gratitude
that has come with it—

the thankfulness that sits
among the sorrow
and can barely begin
to tell you
what it means
not to be alone.

This blessing
knows the distances
you crossed
in person,
in prayer,
to enter into
days of waiting,
nights of long vigil.

It knows the paths
you traveled
to be here
in the dark.

Even in the shadows,
this blessing
sees more than it can say
and has simply
come to show you
the light
that you have given—

not to return it
to you,
not to reflect it
back to you,
but only to ask you
to open your eyes
and see
the grace of it,
the gift that shines
in this brightness
that you bear.

Written for our family the Christmas after Gary died.

Neidín (Little Nest)

I don't know why
your heart went out
to me—
why it chose
this one
for solace
or how it knew
something of the nesting
that was needed.

But it doesn't do
to question grace—
to turn away from
the opening of
the hand
that clears a path,

that provides space
and light
and time,

that gathers up
what has been torn
beyond mending
and makes of it
a shelter.

So I bless
your feathered heart
and the nesting

that it gave
in a far country
that felt
like home.

I bless the spreading
of wings
that offered the possibility
of flight.

I bless the gift
of refuge
that was not only refuge
but a place from which
to watch the horizon,
to face the far distance
and dream anew
of the life that might
draw near.

WELCOMING BLESSING

When you are lost
in your own life.

When the landscape
you have known
falls away.

When your familiar path
becomes foreign
and you find yourself
a stranger
in the story you had held
most dear.

Then let yourself
be lost.
Let yourself leave
for a place
whose contours
you do not already know,
whose cadences
you have not learned
by heart.
Let yourself land
on a threshold
that mirrors the mystery
of your own
bewildered soul.

It will come
as a surprise,
what arrives
to welcome you
through the door,
making a place for you
at the table
and calling you
by your name.

Let what comes,
come.

Let the glass
be filled.
Let the light
be tended.
Let the hands
lay before you
what will meet you
in your hunger.

Let the laughter.
Let the sweetness
that enters
the sorrow.
Let the solace
that comes
as sustenance
and sudden, unbidden
grace.

For what comes,
offer gladness.
For what greets you
with kindly welcome,
offer thanks.
Offer blessing
for those
who gathered you in
and will not
be forgotten—

those who,
when you were
a stranger,
made a place for you
at the table
and called you
by your name.

The Cure for Sorrow

Because I do not know
any medicine for grief
but to let ourselves
grieve.

Because I do not know
any cure for sorrow
but to let ourselves
sorrow.

Because I do not know
any remedy
but to let the heart break,
to let it fall open, then
to let it fall open
still more.

Because I do not know
how to mend
the unmendable,
unfixable,
unhealable wound
that keeps finding
itself healed
as we tend it,
as we follow
the line of it,
as we let it lead us
on the path
it knows.

Because I do not know
any solace
but to give ourselves
into the love
that will never cease
to find us,
that will never loose
its hold on us,
that will never abandon us
to the sorrow
for which it holds
the cure.

Secret Blessing

This is the blessing
no one can write
for you.

This is the blessing
you will find
for yourself—

tucked into
the crack
in the wall,

scribbled in
the gap
between worlds,

sheltered beneath
the outstretched
wing,

inscribed within
the tender
wound.

Secret blessing,
solace blessing,
soothing blessing,
shadowed blessing.

Blessing that steals
into the clench
of your first.

Blessing that blooms
in your opening
hand.

Blessing that lights
the beckoning
path.

Blessing that sings
your new name
to you.

Blessing of Memory

You were born
remembering this blessing.

It has never
not been with you,
weaving itself daily
through the threads of
each story, each dream,
each word you spoke
or received,
everything you hoped,
each person you loved,
all that you lost
with astonishing sorrow,
all that you welcomed
with unimagined joy.

I tell you,
you bear this blessing
in your bones.

But if the day should come
when you can no longer
bring this blessing
to mind,
we will hold it
for you.
We will remember it
for you.

And when
the time comes,
we will breathe
this blessing to you
at the last,
as you are gathered
into the place
where all that
has been lost
finds its way back
to you,
where all memory
returns to you,
where you know yourself
unforgotten
and entirely welcomed
home.

What the Light Shines Through

Where pain
does not touch you.
Where hurt
does not make its home.
Where despair
does not haunt you.
Where sorrow
does not dwell.

Where disease
does not possess you.
Where death
does not abide.
Where horror
does not hold you.
Where fear
does not raise its head.

Where your wounds
become doorways.
Where your scars
become sacred maps.
Where tears
become pools of gladness.
Where delight
attends your way.

Where every kindness
you have offered
returns to you.

Where each blessing
you have given
makes its way back
to you.
Where every grace
gathers around you.
Where the face of love
mirrors your gaze.

Where you are
what the light
shines through.

WHAT FIRE COMES TO SING IN YOU

Blessings of Hope

STAY

I know how your mind
rushes ahead,
trying to fathom
what could follow this.
What will you do,
where will you go,
how will you live?

You will want
to outrun the grief.
You will want
to keep turning toward
the horizon,
watching for what was lost
to come back,
to return to you
and never leave again.

For now,
hear me when I say
all you need to do
is to still yourself,
is to turn toward one another,
is to stay.

Wait
and see what comes
to fill
the gaping hole
in your chest.

Wait with your hands open
to receive what could never come
except to what is empty
and hollow.

You cannot know it now,
cannot even imagine
what lies ahead,
but I tell you
the day is coming
when breath will
fill your lungs
as it never has before,
and with your own ears
you will hear words
coming to you new
and startling.
You will dream dreams
and you will see the world
ablaze with blessing.

Wait for it.
Still yourself.
Stay.

Blessing the Tools of Grief

You had hardly thought
your heart could be
so claimed,
and so willingly.

Now the heart
that gave itself
with such gladness
finds itself stunned
by its anguish,
abandoned and inhabited
all at the same time
by the absence
that has gathered itself
to you.

It will astonish you
how grief comes
with such purpose
to undo us,
to unmake us
with tools fashioned
so exactly
to its terrible art—

how with such precision
they are fitted for
the rending, flaying,
tearing, unstitching,
unmooring,

unhinging,
undoing
of us.

It is hard to see
from here
how these tools
are the same ones
that will make us again,

this time with
an aching slowness,
a painful pace
so measured we will
hardly perceive it
when it begins
to happen—

the joining that comes
piece to piece
in a pattern
that will never be
the same
but will leave us
inexplicably whole.

Blessing for a Whole Heart

You think
if you could just
imagine it,
that would be a beginning;
that if you could envision
what it would look like,
that would be a step
toward a heart
made whole.

This blessing
is for when
you cannot imagine.

This is for when
it is difficult to dream
of what could lie beyond
the fracture, the rupture,
the cleaving through which
has come a life
you do not recognize
as your own.

When all that inhabits you
feels foreign,
your heart made strange
and beating a broken
and unfamiliar song,
let there come
a word of hope,

a voice that speaks
into the shattering,

reminding you
that who you are
is here,
every shard
somehow holding
the whole of you
that you cannot see
but is taking shape
even now,
every part of you
coming together
in an ancient,
remembered rhythm

that bears you
not toward restoration,
not toward return—
as if you could somehow
become unchanged—
but steadily deeper
into the heart of the one
who has already dreamed you
complete.

Blessing for the Raising of the Dead

And he said, "Young man, I say to you, rise!"
—Luke 7:14

This blessing
does not claim
to raise the dead.

It is not so audacious
as that.

But be sure
it can come
and find you
if you think yourself
beyond all hope,
beyond all remedy;
if you have
laid your bones down
in your exhaustion
and grief,
willing yourself numb.

This blessing
knows its way
through death,
knows the paths
that weave
through decay
and dust.

And while this blessing
does not have the power
to raise you,
it knows how
to reach you.

It will come to you,
sit down
beside you,
look you
in the eye,
and ask
if you want
to live.

It has no illusions.
This blessing knows
it is an awful grace
to be returned
to this world.

Just ask Lazarus,
or the Shunammite's son.
Go to Nain
and ask the widow's boy
whether he had
to think twice
about leaving the quiet,
the stillness;
whether he hesitated
just for a moment
before abandoning the place

where nothing could harm
or disturb.

Ask the risen
if it gave them pause
to choose this life—
not as one thrust into it
like a babe,
unknowing, unasking,
but this time
with intent,
with desire.

Ask them how it feels
to claim this living,
this waking;
to welcome the breath
in your lungs,
the blood
in your veins;
to gladly consent
to hold in your chest
the beating heart
of this broken
and dazzling world.

Blessing for the Longest Night

All throughout these months,
as the shadows
have lengthened,
this blessing has been
gathering itself,
making ready,
preparing for
this night.

It has practiced
walking in the dark,
traveling with
its eyes closed,
feeling its way
by memory,
by touch,
by the pull of the moon
even as it wanes.

So believe me
when I tell you
this blessing will
reach you,
even if you
have not light enough
to read it;
it will find you,
even though you cannot
see it coming.

You will know
the moment of its
arriving
by your release
of the breath
you have held
so long;
a loosening
of the clenching
in your hands,
of the clutch
around your heart;
a thinning
of the darkness
that had drawn itself
around you.

This blessing
does not mean
to take the night away,
but it knows
its hidden roads,
knows the resting spots
along the path,
knows what it means
to travel
in the company
of a friend.

So when
this blessing comes,
take its hand.

Get up.
Set out on the road
you cannot see.

This is the night
when you can trust
that any direction
you go,
you will be walking
toward the dawn.

Blessing for Knowing

To receive this blessing,
it might feel like
you are peeling back
every layer of flesh,
exposing every nerve,
baring each bone
that has kept you upright.

It might seem
every word is written
on the back of
something that your life
depends upon,
that to read this blessing
would mean tearing away
what has helped you
remain intact.

Be at peace.
It will not be
as painful as that,
though I cannot say
it will be easy
to accept this blessing,
written as it is
upon your true frame,
inscribed on the skin
you were born
to live in.

The habits that keep you
from yourself,
the misconceptions
others have of you,
the unquestioned limits
you have allowed,
the smallness you have
squeezed yourself into:

these are not
who you are.

This blessing wants
all this to fall away.

This blessing—
and it is stubborn on this point,
I assure you—
desires you to know yourself
as it knows you,
to let go of every layer
that is not you,
to release each thing
you hide behind,
to open your eyes
and see what it sees:

how this blessing
has blazed in you
since before you were born;
how it has sustained you
when you could not see it;

how it haunts you,
prickling beneath your skin,
asking to shine forth
in full and unstinting
measure;
how it begins
and ends with
your true name.

Blessing That Holds a Nest in Its Branches

The emptiness
that you have been holding
for such a long season now;

the ache in your chest
that goes with you
night and day
in your sleeping,
your rising—

think of this
not as a mere hollow,
the void left from
the life that has leached out
of you.

Think of it like this:
as the space being prepared
for the seed.

Think of it
as your earth that dreams
of the branches
the seed contains.

Think of it
as your heart making ready
to welcome the nest
its branches will hold.

BLESSING OF COURAGE

I cannot say
where it lives,
only that it comes
to the heart
that is open,
to the heart
that asks,
to the heart
that does not turn away.

It can take practice,
days of tugging at
what keeps us bound,
seasons of pushing against
what keeps our dreaming
small.

When it arrives,
it might surprise you
by how quiet it is,
how it moves
with such grace
for possessing
such power.

But you will know it
by the strength
that rises from within you
to meet it,
by the release

of the knot
in the center of
your chest
that suddenly lets go.

You will recognize it
by how still
your fear becomes
as it loosens its grip,
perhaps never quite
leaving you,
but calmly turning
into joy
as you enter the life
that is finally
your own.

BLESSING OF THE GATE

Press your hand
to this blessing,
here along
the side
where you can feel
its seam.

Follow the seam
and you will find
the hinges
on which
this blessing turns.

Feel how
your fingers
catch on them—
top,
bottom,
the slightest pressure
sending the gate
gliding open
in a glad welcome.

Wait, did I say
press your hand
to this blessing?

What I meant was
press your hand
to your heart.

Rest it over that
place in your chest
that has grown
closed and tight,
where the rust,
with its talent
for making decay
appear artful,
has bitten into
what you once
held dear.

Breathe deep.
Press on the knot
and feel how it
begins to give way,
turning upon
the hinge
of your heart.

Notice how it
opens wide
and wider still
as you exhale,

spilling you out
into a realm
where you never dreamed
to go
but cannot now imagine
living this life
without.

Blessing in the Dust

You thought the blessing
would come
in the staying;
in casting your lot
with this place,
these people;
in learning the art
of remaining,
of abiding.

And now you stand
on the threshold
again.
The home you had
hoped for,
had ached for,
is behind you—
not yours, after all.

The clarity comes
as small comfort,
perhaps,
but it comes:
illumination enough
for the next step.

As you go,
may you feel
the full weight
of your gifts

gathered up
in your two hands,
the complete measure
of their grace
in your heart that knows
there is a place
for them,
for the treasure
that you bear.

I promise you
there is a blessing
in the leaving,
in the dust shed
from your shoes
as you walk toward home—

not the one you left
but the one that waits ahead,
the one that already
reaches out for you
in welcome,
in gladness
for the gifts
that none but you
could bring.

BLESSING FOR THE PLACE BETWEEN

*And [Jacob] dreamed that there was a ladder set up
on the earth, the top of it reaching to heaven; and the
angels of God were ascending and descending on it.*
        —Genesis 28:12

When you come
to the place between.

When you have left
what you held
most dear.

When you are traveling
toward the life
you know not.

When you arrive
at the hardest ground.

May it become
for you
a place to rest.

May it become
for you
a place to dream.

May the pain
that has pressed itself
into you

give way
to vision,
to knowing.

May the morning
make of it
an altar,
a path,
a place to begin
again.

THE HARDEST BLESSING

Jesus said to him, "Not seven times, but, I tell you,
seventy-seven times."
                    —Matthew 18:22

If we cannot
lay aside the wound,
then let us say
it will not always
bind us.

Let us say
the damage
will not eternally
determine our path.

Let us say
the line of our life
will not always travel
along the places
we are torn.

Let us say
that forgiveness
can take some practice,
can take some patience,
can take a long
and struggling time.

Let us say
that to offer

the hardest blessing,
we will need
the deepest grace;
that to forgive
the sharpest pain,
we will need
the fiercest love;
that to release
the ancient ache,
we will need
new strength
for every day.

Let us say
the wound
will not be
our final home—

that through it
runs a road,
a way we would not
have chosen
but on which
we will finally see
forgiveness,
so long practiced,
coming toward us,
shining with the joy
so well deserved.

Blessing the Water, the Wine

Jesus said to them, "Fill the jars with water."
    —John 2:7

You thought
you had learned
to live with the empty,
the hollow.

You could place your ear
against the rim
of the vessel
of your life
and hear its ringing echo
with equanimity,
not expecting
any more than this,
not even bothered
to be a bystander
at the feast—
if not delighting
in the celebration,
then at least not
despairing in it.

When the water
rushed into the emptiness,
you were surprised
that you could even feel it,
that you could sense
the sudden drenching

when you thought
all had been poured out.

And then suddenly
the sweetness
that stunned you,
that told you
this was not all,
this was not the end—

that this blessing
was saving the best
for last.

Blessing the Fragments

He told his disciples, "Gather up the fragments
left over, so that nothing may be lost."
　　　—John 6:12

Cup your hands together,
and you will see the shape
this blessing wants to take.
Basket, bowl, vessel:
it cannot help but
hold itself open
to welcome
what comes.

This blessing
knows the secret
of the fragments
that find their way
into its keeping,
the wholeness
that may hide
in what has been
left behind,
the persistence of plenty
where there seemed
only lack.

Look into the hollows
of your hands
and ask
what wants to be
gathered there,

what abundance waits
among the scraps
that come to you,
what feast
will offer itself
from the pieces
that remain.

Blessing of Salt, Blessing of Light

*"You are the salt of the earth. . . . You are the light
of the world."*
          —Matthew 5:13–14

By the time you come
to the end of this blessing,
these words will be barely enough
to fit in the palm of your hand.

But fold your fingers around them
and take them
as an offering,
a sacrament,
a sign.

Touch the words
to your tongue
and taste how
they have traveled
through marrow and bone
to reach you,
how they have passed
through each chamber
of your heart,
how they have come
through the layers
that make up your soul—
the strata of stories
and questions,
longings and
dreams.

Savor the way the words
are not mere residue
or dross,
the bitter leavings
from the refining.

By their taste,
you will know instead
they are the essence,
they are the core,
they are what has come
through the burning,

holding still
the memory of fire
and the imprint of light,
holding the clarity that comes
when all that is not needful
passes away.

So take these words
as a blessing;
touch them
to your mouth
(may you taste)
your eyes
(may you see)
your ears
(may you hear)

and then let them go;
let them fall to earth
where all salt finally returns.

See the path they make
for you,
the path that blazes
inside of you,
lighting the way
ahead of you
that only you
can go.

What Fire Comes to Sing in You

This blessing
had big ideas
about what it wanted
to say,
what it wanted you
to know,
to see.

This blessing wanted
to open your eyes
to the joy that lives
in such strange company
with sorrow—
wanted to make sure
to tell you,
lest you forget,
that no matter how long
it seems absent,
no matter how quiet
it becomes,
joy has never
been far from you,
holding a space
of celebration,
watching for you,
humming as it
keeps vigil.

But now that
it comes time

to speak it—
comes time to
lay these words
on your brow,
your beating heart—
all this blessing
can think to say is

Look—
your life
a candle,
this day
a match.
Strike it and see
what blazes,
what fire comes
to sing in you.

Blessing in the Turning

You have turned my mourning into dancing.
        —Psalm 30:11

May you know
the slow mystery
in which mourning
becomes a dance,
turning you toward
the gladness
that wants to meet you
in your grief.

May comfort
come to enfold you,
not to take away
all sorrow
but to infuse it
with tenderness,
with rest,
with every grace
it has.

May you give yourself
to the rhythms
of joy,
even when your steps
are stumbling,
even when you are
most fragile
and faltering.

May you know
the dancing that comes
in the dying,
moving you in time with
the heart that
has held you
always,
even when you
could not hear
its beating,
even when you
could not bear
its love.

Blessing for One Already Brave

I do not know how to ask
that you be encompassed now
when there was no protection
for you then,
nothing that stepped between you
and what came with violence
into your home,
your being.

Yet I have seen the blessing
that came after the rending—
how you took what was torn
and made a life
not unmarked by
what had passed before,
but not unhinged by it.

You know about doors,
know what depends
upon them,
know the grace that comes
in creating our own
and the power of choosing
how we will cross the thresholds
we never hoped to see.

Now your life spirals you
back around
that passage in your story,
and I see you choosing again

to create your own way,
to stand with courage
before this door
and make it your own.

I am stubborn in asking for it:
that when you walk through
you will be encompassed,
that you will be enfolded,
that you will feel the sacred weight
of every word of blessing
we could ever think to offer,

as if each syllable
were inscribed upon you,
you who show us
what being brave looks like—
that it wears
your beloved face.

Blessing of Hope

So may we know
the hope
that is not just
for someday
but for this day—
here, now,
in this moment
that opens to us:

hope not made
of wishes
but of substance,

hope made of sinew
and muscle
and bone,

hope that has breath
and a beating heart,

hope that will not
keep quiet
and be polite,

hope that knows
how to holler
when it is called for,

hope that knows
how to sing

when there seems
little cause,

hope that raises us
from the dead—

not someday
but this day,
every day,
again and
again and
again.

Blessing for an Anniversary Date

I am imagining
you have learned by now
that time will never move
quite straight for you again—
no more forward only,
if ever it traveled that way.

Now it will be
the bend and
the turn of it,
the curve and
the cradling of it,

the unfurling,
unfolding,
unwinding of it
as it arcs you around
in this spiral
of seasons,
as it draws you around
in this circle
of days.

Like today,
for instance—
this day that marks
a year since last
you passed by
this gate,
this threshold,

this door
that lives with such
vividness in your
memory,
opening onto the
chamber of your heart
where what this day once held
keeps happening.

Let yourself listen
for the liturgy
that persists here,
for the life you shared
that still opens out
along secret paths.

Let yourself
linger again
at the door
of this day.

Let yourself
give yourself into
its hours with
exquisite kindness
and wondrous care.

Light the candles
in celebration
of what remains,
in the ceremony
of what abides

in the shelter
of these hours,
in the mystery
of this day.

Blessing That Does Not End

From the moment
it first laid eyes
on you,
this blessing loved you.

This blessing
knew you
from the start.

It cannot explain how.

It just knows
that the first time
it sat down beside you,
it entered into a conversation
that had already been going on
forever.

Believe this conversation
has not stopped.

Believe this love
still lives—
the love that crossed
an impossible distance
to reach you,
to find you,
to take your face
into its hands
and bless you.

Believe this
does not end—
that the gesture,
once enacted,
endures.

Believe this love
goes on—
that it still
takes your face
into its hands,
that it presses
its forehead to yours
as it speaks to you
in undying words,
that it has never ceased
to gather your heart
into its heart.

Believe this blessing
abides.
Believe it goes with you
always.
Believe it knows you
still.

Now, Beloved, We Live

Now, beloved, we live
in a country that has
no name.

No ceremony
for the vows
we make now,
no liturgy for
how wedded,
no ritual for
our marriage
whose only shape
is this:

I hold your heart
in my heart
that you hold.

Never not in
my bones.
Never not in
my blood.

I hold your heart
in my heart
that you hold.

Gathered
without measure,
given back
without reserve.

I hold your heart
in my heart
that you hold.

Mystery, all,
for which I see
no end but that

I hold your heart
in my heart
that you hold.

Blessed, beloved,
in this country that has
no name.

I hold your heart
in my heart
that you hold.

Postscript

Is there a cure for sorrow? At its deepest, grief can make it difficult to believe that we will ever be whole again, that we will ever know joy again, or that hope will ever visit us again. It can leave us believing we will feel this way forever. Yet grief holds strange graces that make it possible to enter into the wholeness that God continually desires for us, even as we continue to live with the pain of our loss.

If there is any cure for sorrow, the cure will not look like we expect. We often think of a cure as a return to a condition we have once known—that it repairs us in a way that leaves us recognizable to ourselves and others. The reality of grief is that the breakage it brings will not allow us to be put back together in the same way. Our life will never look like it did before sorrow arrived.

Yet there is a healing that comes in our grieving, a redemption that does something other than restore us to the lives we once knew. This healing comes, somewhat paradoxically, in allowing ourselves to give exquisite attention to our grief—to feel it in its terrible fullness instead of ignoring it, to let it speak instead of silencing it, and to allow it to show us a way that we could not find on our own.

Part of the strange mystery of grief is that it holds its own cure. We grieve because we have lost a beloved connection to another person or to a way of being in this world. As we tend the connections that remain—our connection to others, including our beloved dead; our connection to God, even when we feel fury at God for allowing such loss; and our connection to the layers of our own hearts—a wholeness steals in that has the ability to make a home in us even when we still feel broken.

It can sometimes seem our grief is all that connects us to what we have lost. This gives it a perilous potency that can threaten the life that seeks to unfold in us—a life capable of holding both love and sorrow. If we allow grief to do its work, the love that lives within it becomes ever more clear and present to us. In time, the love has a way of overtaking the grief, so that our loving, rather than our grieving, becomes our primary bond to what we have lost.

It is, finally, this love that holds our cure. It is this love that *is* our cure. In the deepest pain that rends us, in the keenest solace that visits us, in the hope that does not release its hold on us, love lives, bearing itself toward us as sorrow's most lasting cure.

About the Author

Jan Richardson is a writer, artist, and ordained minister in the United Methodist Church. She serves as director of The Wellspring Studio, LLC, and makes her home in Florida.

You can find her distinctive artwork, writing, and more at her blogs and websites:

The Painted Prayerbook
paintedprayerbook.com

The Advent Door
adventdoor.com

Jan Richardson Images
janrichardsonimages.com

and

janrichardson.com